DINOWORLD
Tyrannosaurus

GLENN W. STORRS

Kingfisher

NEW YORK

CONTENTS

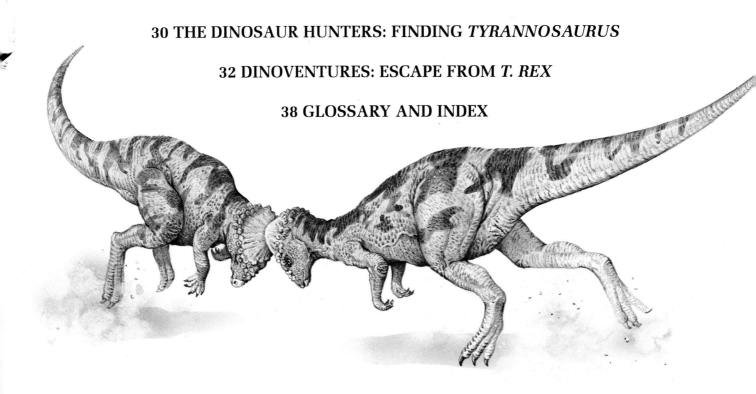

INTRODUCTION

The king of the tyrant lizards, *Tyrannosaurus* must have filled the world with awe and terror as it pursued its prey some 65 million years ago. Those 5-inch-long teeth, with their sharp edges like serrated steak knives, lined the great tyrannosaur jaws, themselves powered by immense muscles. This fearsome apparatus would have sliced through the thickest of dinosaur skin, readily making a meal of just about anything that came too close.

Tyrannosaurus was the largest of meat eaters ever to have lived on land. Up to 40 feet (12 m) in length, it was a bipedal (two-legged) form, charging around the landscape on its hind legs. Its long tail was held well above the ground, waggling from side to side to keep the front end of the animal counterbalanced as it walked or ran. And run it must have, if only to ambush or even chase its next meal. These are clues that come from its hideous teeth and claws, and its strong skeletal build.

But not everything is so obvious about the ways of life for a *Tyrannosaurus*. Despite having very long and powerful hind legs, the arms were exceedingly small, barely able to touch one another, let alone help out with the cutting and slicing. They couldn't even reach its powerhouse of a mouth! Though scientists have known that *Tyrannosaurus* had tiny arms for nearly a century, they still don't know exactly why. Perhaps to help *Tyrannosaurus* rear up from a rest? Or for scratching its stomach? Or perhaps to somehow compensate for having such a large head?

Another puzzler is how such a large, predatory animal, with its massive legs, small arms, and long tail, could be related to the robins, pigeons, and ostriches of today. Yet it is true. While not brothers and sisters, or fathers and mothers to birds, meat-eating dinosaurs, including *Tyrannosaurus* and *Deinonychus*, can be considered the closest of cousins in the genealogy of our feathered fliers. How we are confident that this is true—as well as other facts and fancies about its life and times—is revealed here in this comprehensive overview of *Tyrannosaurus*.

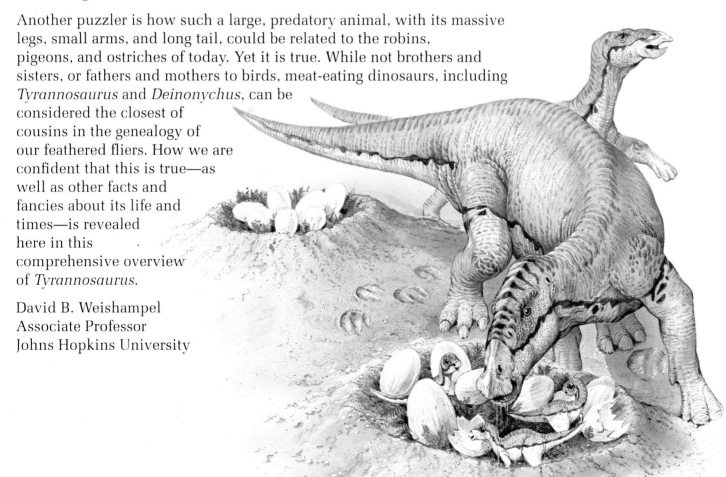

David B. Weishampel
Associate Professor
Johns Hopkins University

A DINOSAUR TIMELINE

The late Cretaceous, which ended about 65 million years ago, produced many new dinosaur species, among them the giant theropod *Tyrannosaurus*. The dinosaurs of the Jurassic had given way to other groups. The sauropods were now rare, and the most common plant eaters were the hadrosaurs like *Edmontosaurus*. Dinosaurs such as *Triceratops* and *Ankylosaurus* evolved spectacular defensive armor and weaponry. Pachycephalosaurs like *Stegoceras*, and ornithomimids such as *Gallimimus*, appeared for the first time.

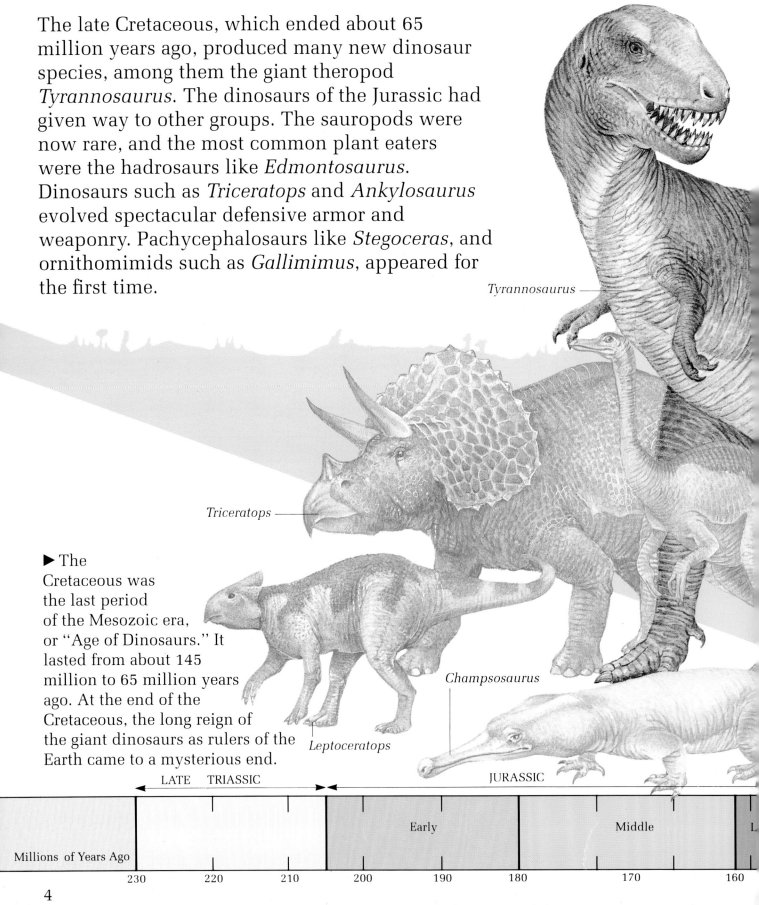

Tyrannosaurus —

Triceratops —

Champsosaurus

Leptoceratops

► The Cretaceous was the last period of the Mesozoic era, or "Age of Dinosaurs." It lasted from about 145 million to 65 million years ago. At the end of the Cretaceous, the long reign of the giant dinosaurs as rulers of the Earth came to a mysterious end.

LATE   TRIASSIC   JURASSIC

				Early			Middle	L

Millions of Years Ago

230   220   210   200   190   180   170   160

▼ The late Cretaceous dinosaur faunas were dominated by herds of the duckbilled hadrosaurs, such as *Edmontosaurus*. *Tyrannosaurus* probably hunted these animals, while its cousin *Ornithomimus* searched for smaller game. Horned dinosaurs ranged from the small *Leptoceratops* to the huge *Triceratops*. Armored dinosaurs such as *Ankylosaurus* were relatively rare. The crocodilelike *Champsosaurus* was not a dinosaur but lived in nearby rivers.

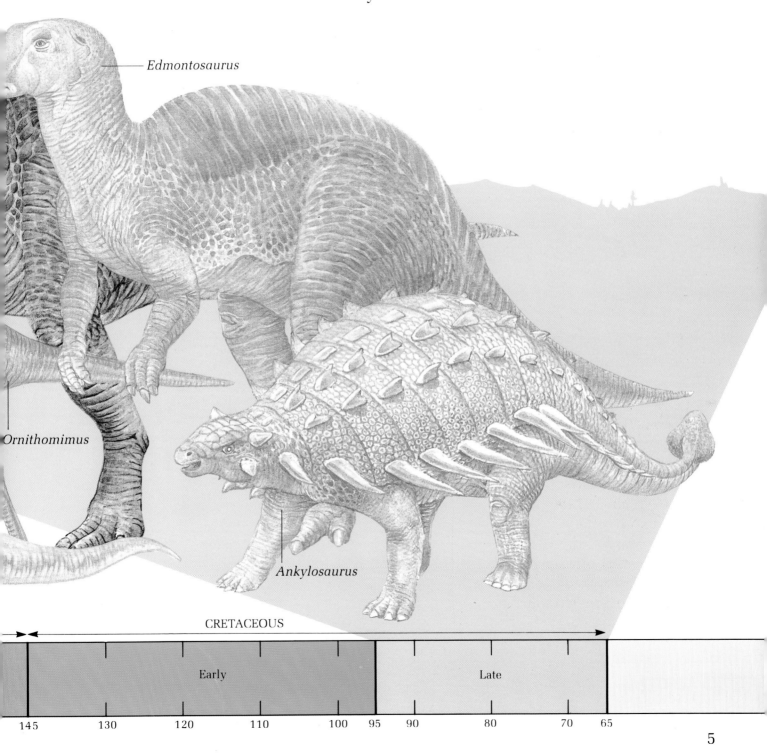

—— *Edmontosaurus*

Ornithomimus

Ankylosaurus

CRETACEOUS

Early

Late

145   130   120   110   100   95   90   80   70   65

70 MILLION YEARS AGO

By the late Cretaceous, the world's continents were nearly in their present positions, but western North America was connected to Asia. Warm seas covered many lands that are now dry. North America was divided by a shallow sea, stretching from the Arctic Ocean to the Gulf of Mexico. Rivers ran from the rising mountains into the sea. In the nearby woodlands lurked *Tyrannosaurus*.

▼ The climate was moderate over most of the world. It was warm in the Arctic. Great herds of duckbills migrated from the dark polar winters, returning north again in the summers.

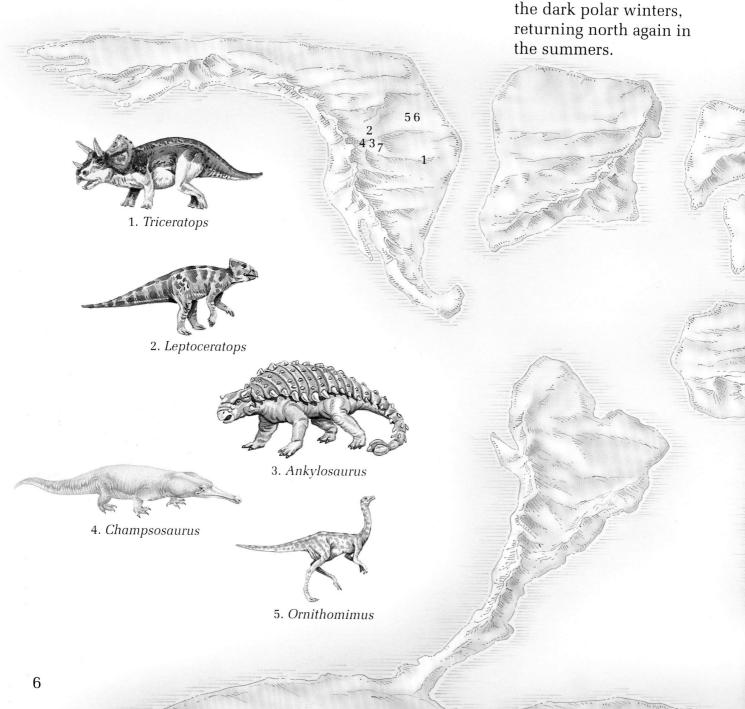

1. *Triceratops*

2. *Leptoceratops*

3. *Ankylosaurus*

4. *Champsosaurus*

5. *Ornithomimus*

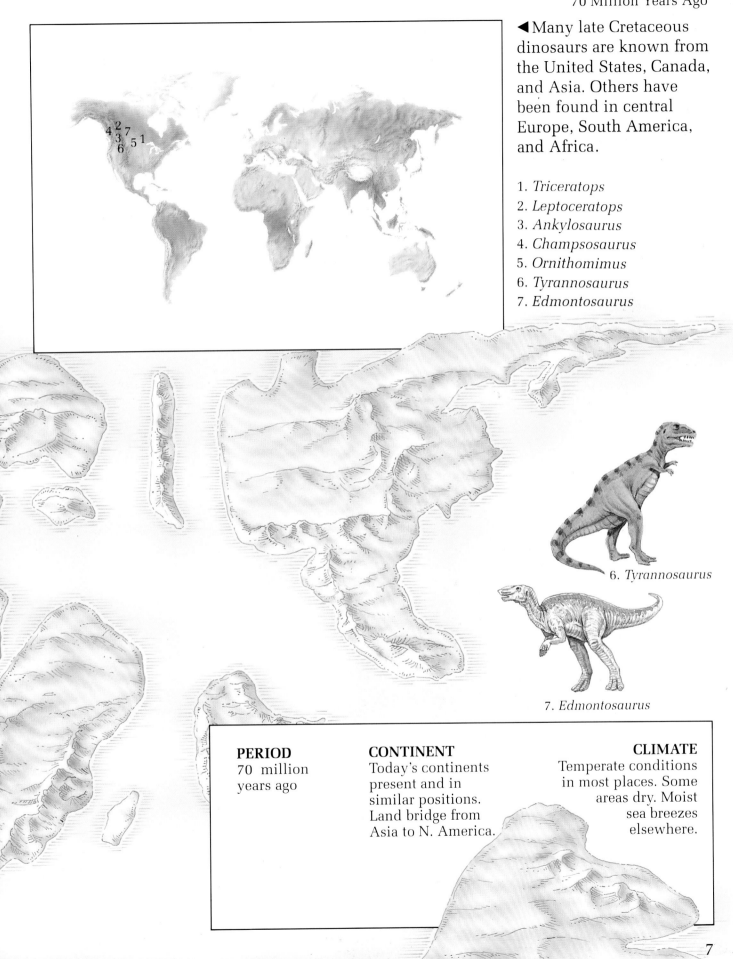

◀Many late Cretaceous dinosaurs are known from the United States, Canada, and Asia. Others have been found in central Europe, South America, and Africa.

1. *Triceratops*
2. *Leptoceratops*
3. *Ankylosaurus*
4. *Champsosaurus*
5. *Ornithomimus*
6. *Tyrannosaurus*
7. *Edmontosaurus*

6. *Tyrannosaurus*

7. *Edmontosaurus*

PERIOD
70 million years ago

CONTINENT
Today's continents present and in similar positions. Land bridge from Asia to N. America.

CLIMATE
Temperate conditions in most places. Some areas dry. Moist sea breezes elsewhere.

7

DELTA DAWN

Tyrannosaurus was first discovered in late Cretaceous rocks of Montana. These rocks, the Hell Creek Formation, represent ancient rivers and streams, and the large deltas that they built out into the sea. Tall evergreen trees and flowering shrubs grew in the sandy flats of the deltas. Sea breezes cooled the warm night air.

▼ Great dinosaur herds roamed the plains between broad rivers. Some of these were duckbill herds, others horned dinosaur herds.

◄ Great flying reptiles may have scavenged on the bodies of dead dinosaurs, like vultures. This is the cycle of life and death.

▼ The tall conifer tree forests of the late Cretaceous deltas were home to many animals. The trees provided their food and shelter.

▼ Volcanic mountains began to grow in the region where the Rocky Mountains now stand.

◄ *Tyrannosaurus*, the giant hunter, lurked among the shadows of the trees, searching for living or dead prey.

▲ Many modern trees had now evolved. Early sycamores, poplars, and dogwoods left their leaves as fossil imprints in the rocks.

▲ Ankylosaurs, such as *Ankylosaurus*, developed heavy armor for protection from giant theropods. The ankylosaurs were cousins of the Jurassic stegosaurs.

ANIMALS OF HELL CREEK

Today, Hell Creek, Montana, is a desert with sage brush and scorpions. Seventy million years ago, it was wet and forested, and full of life. This was the end of the "Age of Dinosaurs," when dinosaurs ruled the Earth. Other animals shared this world, however, some of which would be familiar to us today, others that would seem quite strange. Pterosaurs became giants of the air, while the early mammals were small and secretive. Birds and fish were plentiful. Many of the animal groups that live today had not yet evolved, but the plants of the late Cretaceous were very much like the plants that exist today.

Pterosaurs

The giant pterosaur *Quetzalcoatlus* was a flying reptile, the size of a small airplane.

Plants

Flowering plants were part of the Cretaceous scene. Magnolias, dogwoods, and colorful shrubs attracted the attention of nectar-seeking insects.

Mammals

Marsupials, like *Alphadon*, reared their babies in pouches. Insect eaters, such as *Gypsonictops*, were shrewlike.

Alphadon

Gypsonictops

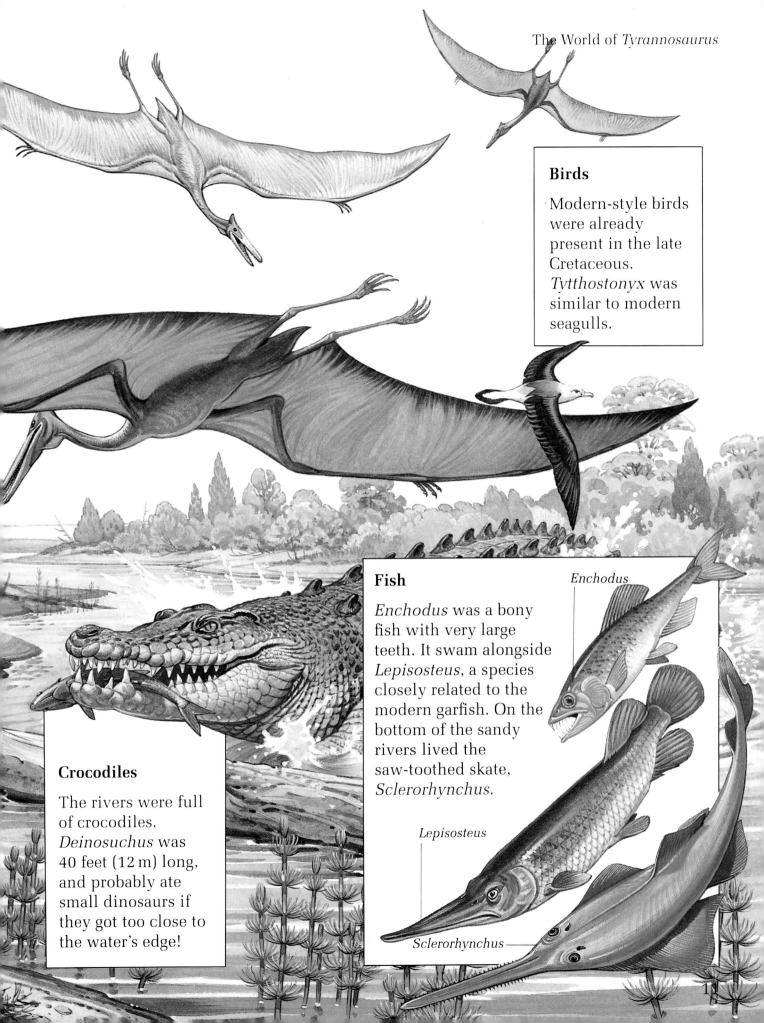

Birds

Modern-style birds were already present in the late Cretaceous. *Tytthostonyx* was similar to modern seagulls.

Fish

Enchodus was a bony fish with very large teeth. It swam alongside *Lepisosteus*, a species closely related to the modern garfish. On the bottom of the sandy rivers lived the saw-toothed skate, *Sclerorhynchus*.

Enchodus

Lepisosteus

Sclerorhynchus

Crocodiles

The rivers were full of crocodiles. *Deinosuchus* was 40 feet (12 m) long, and probably ate small dinosaurs if they got too close to the water's edge!

11

PEACEFUL NEIGHBORS

The giant theropod, *Tyrannosaurus*, lived in a world full of dinosaurs, many of them plant eaters living in fear of hungry tyrannosaurs. Paleontologists are piecing together the lives of these dinosaurs. Most dinosaurs were not slow and stupid, but active agile creatures. Some probably had structured family lives and complex behavior. The hadrosaurs, or duckbills, for instance, apparently lived in great herds and looked after their young while they were in the nest. Pachycephalosaurs may have competed with rivals for the attention of a mate. They seem to have butted their thick-skulled heads together, in the same way that rams do today.

Edmontosaurus

ed-MONT-oh-SAW-rus
"EDMONTON REPTILE"
42 FT. 6 IN. (13 M) LONG

A very common duckbilled hadrosaur.

Nest

Young *Edmontosaurus*

Eggs

Pachycephalosaurus

pak-ee-SEF-a-loh-
SAW-rus
"THICKHEADED
REPTILE"
15 FT. (4.6 M) LONG

A boneheaded
dinosaur.

Ornithomimus

or-NITH-oh-MIME-us
"BIRD MIMIC"
11 FT. 6 IN. (3.5 M) LONG

This may have eaten
eggs and small
animals.

DIFFICULT DINNERS

Tyrannosaurus was a carnivorous (meat-eating) theropod and killed other dinosaurs for food. It is the largest known carnivore, and must have been a fearsome enemy. Many late Cretaceous dinosaurs, however, were well equipped to withstand the attacks of *Tyrannosaurus*. Some, like the ankylosaurs and their cousins the nodosaurs, had heavy armor for protection. Others had weapons of their own, such as clubs and horns, that could injure, cripple, or perhaps kill a hungry attacker. The horned ceratopsians had the most obvious defensive weaponry. No wonder that *Tyrannosaurus* probably preferred easier game.

Euoplocephalus

yu-OP-lo-SEF-a-lus
"WELL-ARMORED HEAD"
23 FT. (7 M) LONG

Many ankylosaurs had a heavy bony club at the end of the tail. A blow from this club could cripple a giant predator.

Panoplosaurus

pan-OH-plo-SAW-rus
"FULLY-ARMORED REPTILE"
23 FT. (7 M) LONG

This armored nodosaur was well protected from enemies.

Triceratops

try-SAIR-a-tops
"THREE-HORNED FACE"
30 FT. (9 M) LONG

The horned dinosaurs were unique to the Cretaceous and were formidable adversaries. With its three great horns, *Triceratops* might counter *Tyrannosaurus* with a direct charge.

KING OF THE CRETACEOUS

Tyrannosaurus means "tyrant reptile," and it must certainly have been the lord of all it surveyed. It was the last and largest "carnosaur," or giant carnivorous dinosaur, growing up to 40 feet (12 m) long, and it had no natural enemies. This spectacular animal, in spite of its tremendous size and huge toothed jaws, had hollow bones, three prominent toes, and a bipedal (two-legged) stance —all characteristics shared with its smaller cousins the birds! It has even been suggested that it was warm-blooded, like birds, but we may never know if this was true because only *Tyrannosaurus* bones and teeth have been preserved.

▼ Few intact skeletons of *Tyrannosaurus* have been found. Nevertheless, they give us a complete picture of this dinosaur's appearance.

Tail vertebrae

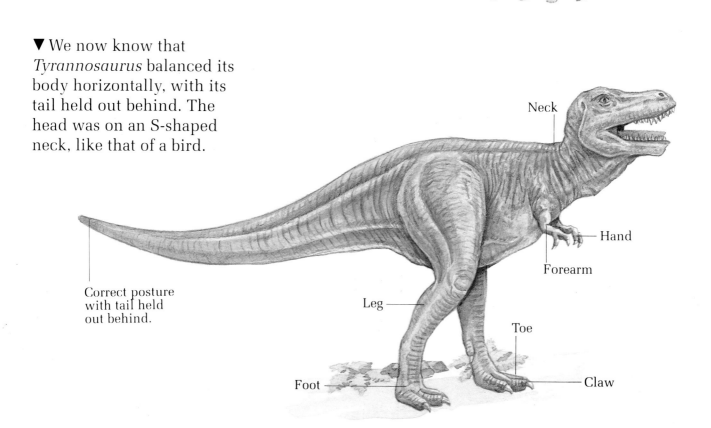

▼ We now know that *Tyrannosaurus* balanced its body horizontally, with its tail held out behind. The head was on an S-shaped neck, like that of a bird.

Neck

Hand

Forearm

Correct posture with tail held out behind.

Leg

Toe

Foot

Claw

16

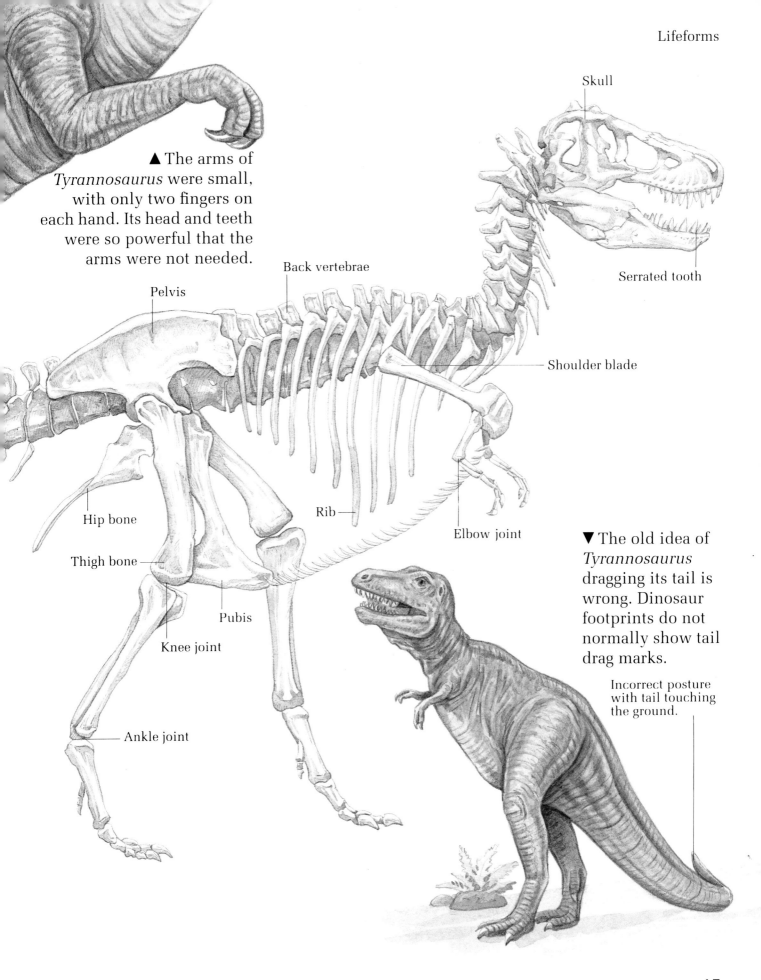

▲ The arms of *Tyrannosaurus* were small, with only two fingers on each hand. Its head and teeth were so powerful that the arms were not needed.

Skull

Serrated tooth

Back vertebrae

Pelvis

Shoulder blade

Hip bone

Rib

Elbow joint

Thigh bone

▼ The old idea of *Tyrannosaurus* dragging its tail is wrong. Dinosaur footprints do not normally show tail drag marks.

Pubis

Knee joint

Incorrect posture with tail touching the ground.

Ankle joint

MAKING A LIVING

It is clear from its teeth that *Tyrannosaurus* ate meat, but did it actually hunt and kill its own food? Some people have suggested that it only fed off the carcasses of animals that were already dead, perhaps because it was too big and slow to chase other dinosaurs. In fact, *Tyrannosaurus*'s strong jaw muscles, long sharp teeth, powerful legs, large claws, and relatively big brain show that it was surely able to kill for itself.

Tyrannosaurus was certainly a successful predator. Perhaps it did not need to be terribly fast, for it may have ambushed unsuspecting dinosaurs by springing out from a concealed position—although such a big dinosaur would be hard to hide!

▼ The feet of *Tyrannosaurus* were perfectly made for supporting its bulky body. The splayed toes and large claws spread the animal's weight.

Toe

Claw

Corythosaurus

kor-ITH-oh-SAW-rus
"HELMETED REPTILE"
33 FT. (10 M) LONG

A lambeosaurine duckbill.

TOOLS OF THE TRADE

The massive head of *Tyrannosaurus* had a wide and gaping mouth, full of steak-knife teeth. It could cut out and swallow huge chunks of meat without chewing. The teeth were up to 6 inches (15 cm) long, and had sharp cutting edges, with sawlike serrations. These teeth were constantly replaced, as old teeth wore down and fell out.

A *Tyrannosaurus* tooth

▼ *Tyrannosaurus* could certainly scavenge its food. Such a large dinosaur could easily have taken food from other animals. The smell of a fresh kill might have attracted tyrannosaurs from far and wide.

RUNNING THE RACE

How did *Tyrannosaurus* move? Was it big and slow, or did it run quickly? Its bones give us some clues. The proportions of its limbs suggest that it was a quick, agile animal, but not one with great speed. Its broad, birdlike feet provided good balance, but its long thigh bone shows that it could not move its legs very rapidly. Probably, *Tyrannosaurus* could chase its prey, but only catch the weakest and slowest animals. Certainly, *Tyrannosaurus* did not have to run *away* from anything!

◀ The old idea of *Tyrannosaurus* as an ungainly, lumbering monster—slow and clumsy, and unable to catch its own food—is certainly wrong. It was built to hunt.

▼ *Tyrannosaurus* was probably very birdlike in its movements. It could run, but was certainly not very fast—not as fast as a horse, for example.

Footprints of a large, three-toed dinosaur

▼ Fossil footprints of dinosaurs give the paleontologist an idea of their movement and behavior. Measuring the gaps between them gives an estimate of speed, once we know the dinosaur's approximate height.

21

NEXT MEAL

When *Tyrannosaurus* was on the prowl, there was no lack of other dinosaurs to eat, but not all were easy to kill. Because so many late Cretaceous dinosaurs had evolved strong defenses against predators, *Tyrannosaurus* probably often ate duck-billed hadrosaurs. They were plentiful, and had no horns or bony armor for protection. Perhaps the duckbills formed the biggest part, if not all, of a tyrannosaur's diet. All hadrosaurs were herbivores (plant eaters).

▼ Without natural defenses of its own, the hadrosaur's back was vulnerable to the bite of a tyrannosaur. We often find tyrannosaur teeth in hadrosaur bones.

▶ One of the most common Cretaceous dinosaurs was *Edmontosaurus*. Like other hadrosaurs, it had a broad duck-like bill, with which it cropped conifer needles and other plant food.

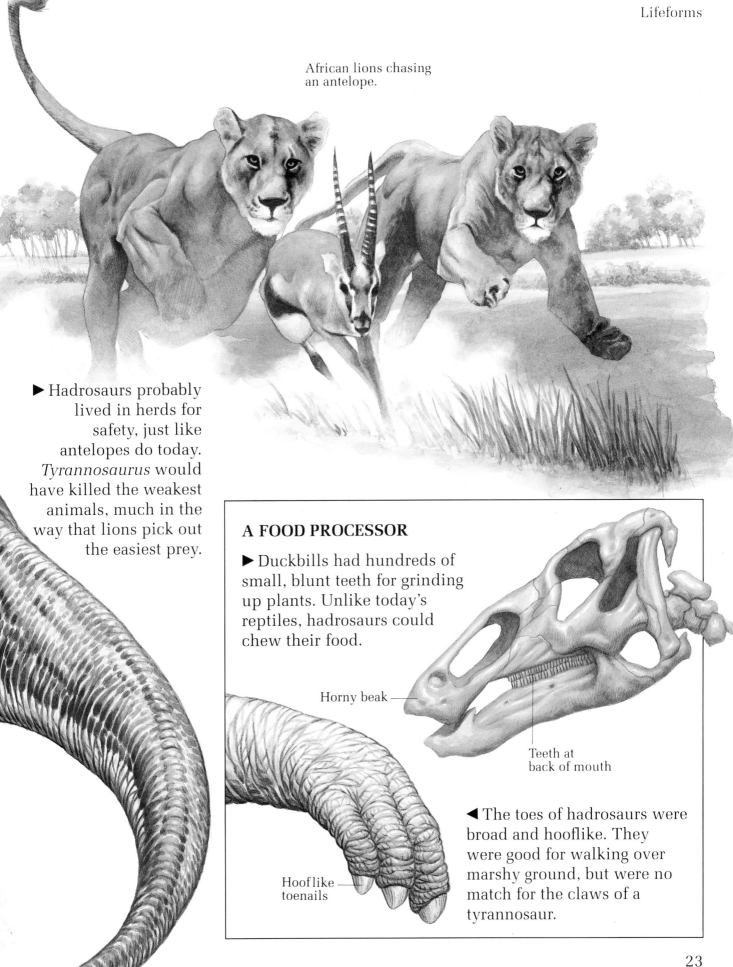

African lions chasing an antelope.

▶ Hadrosaurs probably lived in herds for safety, just like antelopes do today. *Tyrannosaurus* would have killed the weakest animals, much in the way that lions pick out the easiest prey.

A FOOD PROCESSOR

▶ Duckbills had hundreds of small, blunt teeth for grinding up plants. Unlike today's reptiles, hadrosaurs could chew their food.

Horny beak

Teeth at back of mouth

◀ The toes of hadrosaurs were broad and hooflike. They were good for walking over marshy ground, but were no match for the claws of a tyrannosaur.

Hooflike toenails

THE TYRANNOSAUR FAMILY

Tyrannosaurus was one of several similar dinosaurs, although it was the largest tyrannosaur, and is the most famous. Tyrannosaurs are so far known only from the late Cretaceous period of North America and Asia. They were the last in a long line of giant meat eaters, which began in the Triassic age with small forms like *Coelophysis*, and included *Allosaurus* from the Jurassic. The tyrannosaur family mysteriously became extinct with all other large dinosaurs (leaving only avian theropods—the birds) at the end of the Cretaceous period.

Nanotyrannus

NAN-oh-tie-RAN-us
"DWARF TYRANT"
16 FT. (5 M) LONG

This recently discovered tyrannosaur is from Montana.

Tyrannosaurus

tie-RAN-oh-SAW-rus
"TYRANT REPTILE"
40 FT. (12 M) LONG

The most famous tyrannosaur was also the largest.

Tarbosaurus

TARB-oh-SAW-rus
"ALARMING REPTILE"
33 FT. (10 M) LONG

A smaller cousin of *Tyrannosaurus*, from Mongolia in Asia.

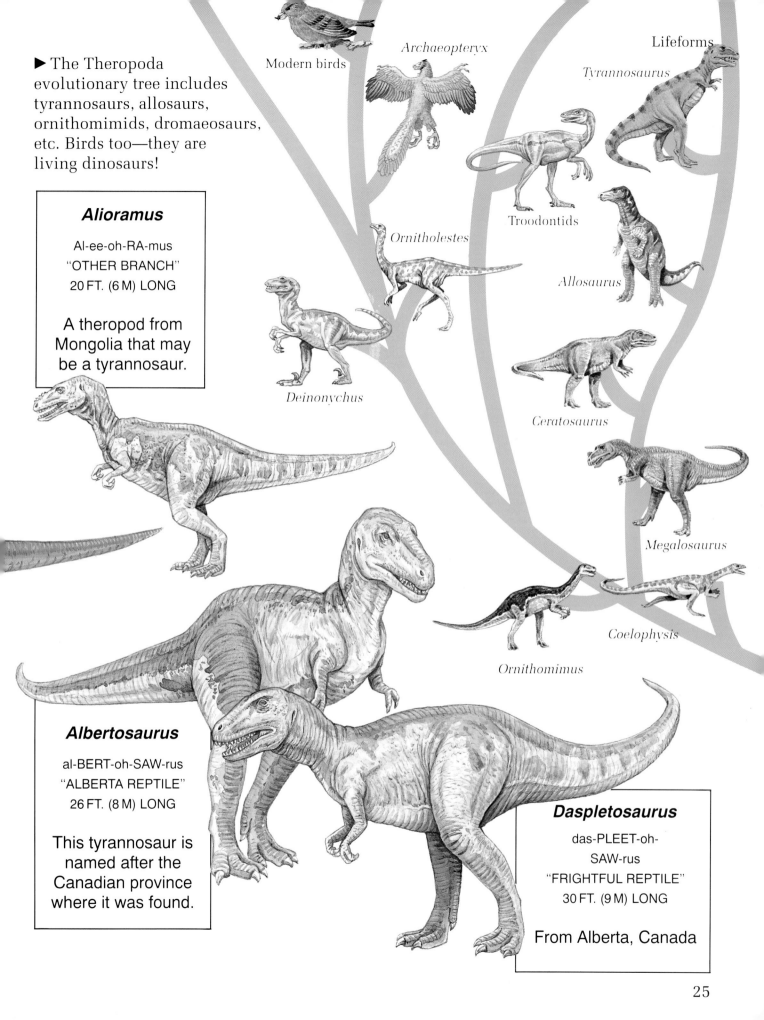

▶ The Theropoda evolutionary tree includes tyrannosaurs, allosaurs, ornithomimids, dromaeosaurs, etc. Birds too—they are living dinosaurs!

Modern birds

Archaeopteryx

Lifeforms

Tyrannosaurus

Troodontids

Ornitholestes

Allosaurus

Deinonychus

Ceratosaurus

Megalosaurus

Coelophysis

Ornithomimus

Alioramus

Al-ee-oh-RA-mus
"OTHER BRANCH"
20 FT. (6 M) LONG

A theropod from Mongolia that may be a tyrannosaur.

Albertosaurus

al-BERT-oh-SAW-rus
"ALBERTA REPTILE"
26 FT. (8 M) LONG

This tyrannosaur is named after the Canadian province where it was found.

Daspletosaurus

das-PLEET-oh-SAW-rus
"FRIGHTFUL REPTILE"
30 FT. (9 M) LONG

From Alberta, Canada

TOWARD EXTINCTION

All the giant dinosaurs became extinct at or near the end of the late Cretaceous period, about 65 million years ago. No one knows why, although there have been many theories. Some of the old ideas are outrageously fanciful. For instance, it has been suggested that the dinosaurs were killed by poisonous air, a lack of minerals, cosmic radiation, floods, sunspots, volcanoes, overeating, or over population. It was even said that dinosaurs were too stupid to survive—even though they existed for over 150 million years! When we talk about why the dinosaurs became extinct, it's worth noting that human beings have only been around for about two million years.

▼ A once popular idea was that drought, starvation, and disease killed the dinosaurs. The climate and environment of the world are always changing, but did they change so suddenly that dinosaurs could not cope?

▼ A silly notion to explain the extinction is that the food supply became poisonous. Although many plants have toxins for defense against herbivores, dinosaurs would have avoided inedible plants.

◄ *Parasaurolophus*, was a very successful plant eater. There is no evidence at all to think that it was killed by its food!

► Did small mammals eat too many of the dinosaurs' eggs? No baby dinosaurs would mean eventual extinction. This is obviously incorrect, because the dinosaurs and early mammals coexisted for millions of years.

DINOFACTS

Q: How can you tell the difference between a male and female *Tyrannosaurus*?

▼ We can tell the difference between a female and male mallard duck by their different-colored plumage.

Female mallard

Male mallard

A: This is very hard to do from fossils. Maybe a very large *Tyrannosaurus* skeleton would be that of a male, while the female was smaller, or vice versa. In many modern reptiles and birds the female is often larger than her mate. Also, the sexes of some animals today, especially birds, are different colors. Perhaps the color of *Tyrannosaurus* was different in males and females. A new theory suggests that the bones at the base of the tail were different to allow for the passage of eggs.

Q: Has a complete *Tyrannosaurus* fossil ever been found?

A: A new *Tyrannosaurus* skeleton was recently discovered in Montana. It is one of the most complete and biggest examples ever found of this dinosaur. It is now being studied by scientists at the Museum of the Rockies, at Bozeman, Montana. Yet another new *Tyrannosaurus* from South Dakota, is now the object of an ownership dispute in the courts. Unfortunately, fossils have become big business.

Q: How big was *Tyrannosaurus*?

A: This would depend on the age and sex of an individual. Just as in animals today, dinosaurs came in a variety of sizes. Naturally, the young animals would have been smaller than adults. Also, male dinosaurs may have been larger than the females, or vice versa. Of course, even two adults might be different in size. The largest *Tyrannosaurus* was probably about 40 feet (12 m) long.

Q: How much did *Tyrannosaurus* weigh?

A: We can estimate the weight of a dinosaur from its size while alive. Because animals are made up mostly of water, they weigh only a little less than the same amount of water. If we make a lifelike model of a dinosaur, we will know the amount of water it equals, by the amount it will displace in a measured container. It is then easy to scale the estimate up to full size. Because an adult *Tyrannosaurus* was so big, it may have weighed 5 or 6 tons.

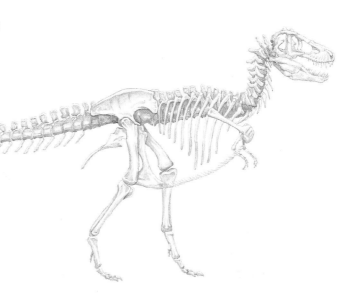

▲ Complete dinosaur skeletons are very rare, so a new *Tyrannosaurus* will give us lots of new information.

Q: Why was *Tyrannosaurus* so vicious?

A: It is wrong to say that this was a vicious animal. It made its living by being a hunter and was only good at its job! Various organisms obtain food in many different ways. Some animals, such as *Tyrannosaurus*, eat meat, and they must be good hunters to survive. *Tyrannosaurus* had very efficient hunting tools in its teeth and certainly must have seemed ferocious, but it did not kill out of spite.

▼ This *Edmontosaurus* died of natural causes, but some skeletons contain theropod teeth, showing they were eaten.

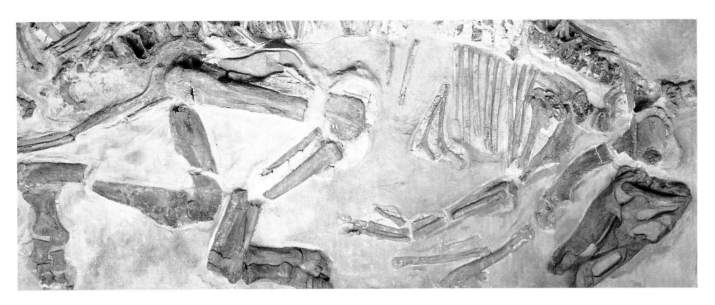

Q: When was the last *Tyrannosaurus* alive?

A: The last one died at the close of the Cretaceous period. It is still a mystery why such dinosaurs disappeared. If, as some scientists think, they were killed by an asteroid or comet hitting the Earth, *Tyrannosaurus* was just unlucky.

▶ The meteor crater at Wolf Creek, Australia, is one of the largest in the world. It shows the tremendous power potential of extra-terrestrial objects.

FINDING *TYRANNOSAURU*

The first *Tyrannosaurus* was discovered in 1902, by Barnum Brown of the American Museum of Natural History. He traveled from New York to prospect for dinosaurs in Montana. His boss was the celebrated paleontologist Henry F. Osborn, who described the new fossil skeleton, and gave it the famous name everyone knows today. Montana is a particularly good place to find dinosaur fossils, because many of the rocks there are of the right age, are river and delta sediments where dinosaurs lived, and are well exposed in desert "badlands."

▶ A *Tyrannosaurus* skeleton, erected at the museum, has fascinated generations of schoolchildren. It even inspired some of them to become paleontologists!

◀ Barnum Brown (hammer in hand) collects a dinosaur leg bone with H. F. Osborn. You can see that the landscape (at Como Bluff) is dry and barren.

▼ Traditional methods of collecting dinosaurs relied on horses, wagons, and manual labor. Today, we use off-road vehicles, jackhammers, and much more—sometimes even helicopters. Brute force and hard work, however, will never be obsolete!

ESCAPE FROM *T. REX*

All known facts about dinosaurs and their habitats have been entered into a computer program called DINO, designed by world-famous paleontologist Dr. Karl Harlow. He has linked this up to a Virtual Reality machine, with controls that allow the operators to move through the computer-generated landscapes, as though they are living dinosaurs themselves. Dr. Harlow has devised a number of "games" that will allow him to observe how dinosaurs may have behaved under certain circumstances. To this, he has added something called the "Random Effect"—unpredictable consequences caused by the presence of the player in the game. The players are his children: Buddy, a thirteen-year-old girl, who is brilliant at computer games, and Rob, her ten-year-old brother, who is mad about dinosaurs and wants to be a paleontologist. When "playing" DINO, Buddy and Rob will have to get as close to the "Virtual" dinosaurs as possible. They may even have to kill to survive, or become hunted themselves and risk "death by dinosaur!"

The computer had selected Buddy to enter DINO for the one role she dreaded most—to observe and possibly confront Tyrannosaurus rex. As with all impressionable children, Buddy had held T. rex in total awe since she was very small. She remembered the toys both she and Rob had enjoyed as kids. These were hard rubber monsters, crudely painted with blood-splashed jaws, plastic transformers with batteries that powered flashing red eyes, and a soft cuddly T. rex with button eyes and a stupid grin. She remembered the toys lined along bookshelves in her bedroom, and felt again the terror when her father switched off the light, and the shadows of her toys, cast by the filtered street lights, reared up and lengthened against the bedroom wall. She had stayed awake some nights, until sheer exhaustion had eased her into sleep.

The VR glove

"If you would prefer not to do this, Buddy, I don't mind if you give *T. rex* a miss. Even in a computer program he is probably best avoided," Karl Harlow had said, as she pulled on the Virtual Reality helmet.

"No Dad. I'm going to meet it face to face," she said, sounding braver than she really felt. It would be like seeing a horror movie, she told herself. *T. rex* could do her no more harm than a TV bug-eyed monster. But she knew that Virtual Reality was very different from sitting in an armchair, watching TV in the same room as your family. Very different.

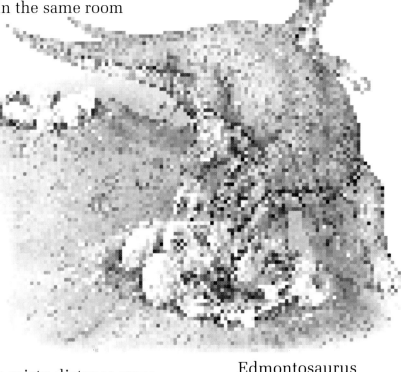

She finished adjusting the VR equipment and said into the small mike: "OK Dad. Ready to meet Mr. Nasty."

"Just getting your BV through. Looks as though you're in luck. It's a Quetz." This was their name for *Quetzalcoatlus*—the gigantic flying pterosaur. In the computer program she would have all its physical abilities. The screensaver of circling *Pteranodon*s faded, and gave way to a breathtaking view ... far below her was an ancient sea, its waves breaking on a late Cretaceous shore. A broad, flat river delta spilled from a vast flood plain. In the misty distance were mountains, wisps of smoke suggesting volcanic activity.

Edmontosaurus
with its young

Buddy—as a *Quetzalcoatlus*—tried her flight controls by moving her fingers in the VR glove. "This is beautiful," she said, as the huge wings of the Quetz dipped, and made her begin a graceful spiraling descent toward the delta and the horrors it held. She began her report: "Somewhere near modern Seattle, visibility good, temperature is 105 degrees Fahrenheit, humidity high. Vegetation is quite a mix: ferns, palms, figs, and sycamores, with groves of magnolias. Selecting DINODATA. Family of *Triceratops* browsing the magnolias directly below me, a herd of *Edmontosaurus* way off to the south, two *Pachycephalosaurus* approaching this area, an *Ankylosaurus* a mile east, and there he is—old Mr. Nasty, an adult *Tyrannosaurus*, one click north of here and approaching. I suddenly feel a bit sick."

Buddy glided over the shimmering waters of the delta, moving the large counterbalanced head of her Quetz Biovehicle in search of her quarry. She saw the *Triceratops* first. It swiveled its head

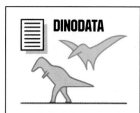

DINODATA

TRICERATOPS
27 feet long.
Bulky body.
Massive head, with
deep parrotlike
beak and neck frill
with bony bumps.

upward as her shadow passed over, and revealed its armored neck frill, edged with a zigzag of bony knobs. Its two massive horns looked terrifyingly sharp. It was quietly and calmly cropping the huge magnolia blooms with its oversized beak of a mouth. "I've found a *Triceratops*," Buddy said into her headset, "Mr. T is probably not far from here. I'm going to take a look." With a few downbeats of those enormous leathery wings, Buddy lifted herself high above the flood plain. Without warning, a *Tyrannosaurus* burst through the magnolias in several enormous

"*T. rex* bounded after her and made a lunge with its teeth-laden head."

ALERT

Year
70 MY

V. Time
06.28

EXIT

RANDOM
EFFECT

ENERGY

strides that shook the ground. Still gliding some 500 feet above this scene, Buddy wheeled in a large circle to see what the *Tyrannosaurus* would do now. It was her mission, after all, to observe and if possible *interact* with the dinosaurs in her program.

From the safety of her airborne observatory, this most feared of all carnosaurs did not seem so terrifying. Its puny arms looked like pipe cleaners, stuck on its body as an afterthought. But as Buddy's shadow passed over it, the *Tyrannosaurus* looked up and opened its vast jaw the width of a child's outstretched arms. This mighty jaw was fringed with teeth like hunting knives, some missing, some broken—all daggers. It uttered its terrible roar of hunger and snapped its jaws together. Buddy shuddered.

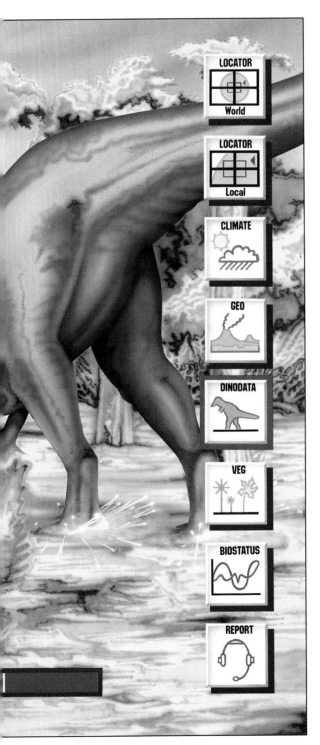

She then realized that the *Triceratops* was still on her screen. Unable to retreat, as there was a wall of rock behind it, the Tric had remained watchful and quiet—its fearsome horns following the *Tyrannosaurus*, wherever it moved. And *T. rex* was now sniffing the air. It knew that meat was nearby, but the Tric was partly concealed by magnolia trees. As Buddy's shadow passed over the Tric, it turned its head upward. The *Tyrannosaurus* caught the movement and swung its rectangular block of a head toward the Tric. With a roar of triumph, *T. rex* bounded with surprising speed through the magnolias and confronted the cornered herbivore. There was a moment of stillness as the two dinosaurs weighed each other up, then, with a roar the *Tyrannosaurus* lunged at the Tric. Buddy saw a flash of teeth, and *T. rex* had the Tric by the neck frill. The Tric violently shook its head and a horn stabbed *T. rex* just below one of its flailing arms. With a bellow of pain and surprise, the *Tyrannosaurus* lifted its great head, and then dropped it like a hammer on the exposed neck of the Tric. It was over quickly. Buddy heard the sound of crunching vertebrae as *T. rex*'s teeth found their mark. The Tric leaned sideways, sunk to its knees, and then fell heavily into the dust. Buddy watched in horror as the *Tyrannosaurus* began to feed on the still dying beast.

Still gliding above this horrific happening on the ground below, Buddy saw a puff of dust followed a second or so later by a loud *crumpf*. Two *Pachycephalosaurus* were performing their ancient ritual of head-to-head duels. They stood about 50 feet apart and pawed the ground, raising dust.

At some unseen signal, each animal rushed at great speed on two birdlike legs toward its oncoming target. The bony heads met with a sharp crack and one animal, clearly stunned, made a wobbly retreat, while the other prepared itself for another attack.

The second charge was interrupted by a thunderous bellow from the *Tyrannosaurus*, who objected to being distracted from its grisly meal. Both of the head bangers, their battle forgotten, crashed through the magnolia grove, and away from Buddy's field of vision.

She was lifted high above the flood plain on a sudden updraught of warm air and felt a wonderful wave of relief at being distanced from *T. rex*'s jaws. Below she spotted the herd of *Edmontosaurus*, disturbed by some unseen predator, stampeding northward across the plain. She mentally willed them not to come too close to the *Tyrannosaurus*. She saw, too, the pair of rival *Pachycephalosaurus*, sizing each other up near a clump of dogwoods. Buddy's observations were interrupted by a flashing warning light—it told her that her energy level was critical. She needed food urgently. Meat, preferably carrion. With a sickening realization she knew exactly where to find it.

Alphadon (left) with *Gypsonictops*

There was but one thing to do. She had to return to the Tric and feed on what remained of it. She just hoped that the *Tyrannosaurus* had moved on. As she glided down to the rocks where the Tric had been savagely killed, Buddy moved her VR helmet from side to side, searching for signs of the *T. rex*. It was nowhere to be seen. She could make out the badly butchered corpse of the Tric. Its rib cage stuck in the air like a huge shopping basket. Buddy floated down and with expert use of her finger controls brought the Quetz to a halt a few feet from the Tric. It was then she understood why the *Quetzalcoatlus* spent so much time in the air—on the ground it was a clumsy contraption. Its enormous wings dragged along behind her, as she tried to hop and crawl the few feet to her energy source.

Buddy closed her mind to what she was doing and fed. She was pleased to see her energy levels rise with each disgusting beakful of *Triceratops* flesh. But her relief was short-lived when she heard the blood-chilling roar of the *Tyrannosaurus*. She felt the ground vibrate with each of its terrible footfalls. It had come to claim its unfinished meal, and Buddy was caught in the act of stealing it. She had to get airborne as quickly as possible. That was her only escape. She hopped off the Tric carcass and loped away from the approaching *Tyrannosaurus*. It bounded after her and made a lunge with its teeth-laden head. It missed, but only by inches. Buddy, even in her terror, knew that *T. rex* was slower than when it had attacked the Tric. As she struggled to open her wings, she remembered to hit the Random Effect control. It might suddenly give the *Tyrannosaurus* extra strength, cause a flood, make a volcano, drop a meteorite—she had no idea. But when she hit the screen menu, the wind strengthened, straightened out her wings, and lifted her off the ground. *T. rex* made a desperate biting jump as she was lifted above it. The teeth snapped together on empty space. She swiveled her electronic head down to see the dying *Tyrannosaurus* slumped on its side, the wound made by the *Triceratops*'s horns now bleeding freely. Numerous *Alphadon*, small omniverous marsupials, were already gathering under nearby trees, to feed upon the greatest meat eater of them all.

"The second charge was interrupted by a thunderous bellow from the *Tyrannosaurus*."

Another warning signal told Buddy she would have to exit from DINO, or lose precious points. She looked down upon the gasping *Tyrannosaurus* with mixed feelings of horror and sadness, her childhood fears finally laid to rest. With her *Quetzalcoatlus*'s claw, she pressed EXIT. The screensaver image returned to tell her she was now out of DINO. Pulling off the VR helmet, she was relieved to see the familiar faces of her brother Rob, and her father, Dr. Harlow. They greeted her as though she had been away for over 70 million years. Which, in a way, she had.

GLOSSARY

Ankylosaur ("stiff reptile"): An armored dinosaur with bony plates and a club at the end of its tail.

Avian: Birdlike, or relating to birds.

Bipedal ("two-footed"): Walking on two legs.

Carnivore ("meat eater"): An animal that eats other animals.

Carnosaur ("meat reptile"): A large carnivorous dinosaur.

Conifer: A type of evergreen tree, usually with cones and needlelike leaves.

Cretaceous ("of the chalk" after the fine limestones then associated with it): The last geological period of the "Age of Dinosaurs" – from about 145 million to 65 million years ago.

Dinosaur ("terrible reptile"): One of a group of advanced reptiles common in the Mesozoic era.

Dromaeosaur ("running reptile"): A birdlike theropod dinosaur with a stiff tail and large toe claws.

Extinction ("wiping out"): The death of a species, or larger group, of animals or plants.

Fauna: The animals of a particular region or period.

Formation: In geology, a large named unit of rock with some common characteristics.

Hadrosaur ("big reptile"): A duckbilled ornithopod dinosaur.

Herbivore ("plant eater"): An animal that eats only plants.

Lambeosaur ("Lambe reptile," after the Canadian paleontologist Lawrence Lambe): A duckbilled dinosaur with a bony crest on its head.

Marsupial: A mammal that rears its young in a pouch on its belly.

Mesozoic ("middle life"): The "Age of Dinosaurs" comprising the Triassic, Jurassic, and Cretaceous geologic periods – from about 245 million to 65 million years ago.

Organism: A living creature, including animals, plants, fungi, and microbes.

Ornithomimid ("bird mimic"): A toothless theropod dinosaur of the dinosaur family Ornithomimidae.

Ornithopod ("bird foot"): Small to medium-sized, plant-eating dinosaur that could stand on two legs and had a stiff tail; includes *Dryosaurus* and the duckbills.

Pachycephalosaur ("thick-headed reptile"): A dome-headed, two-legged plant-eating dinosaur.

Paleontologist ("ancient life studier"): A scientist who studies prehistoric life and its fossil evidence.

Predator: A meat-eating animal that hunts and kills other animals for food.

Pterosaur ("wing reptile"): An extinct flying reptile, with membraned wings. Not a dinosaur.

Sauropod ("reptile foot"): A giant, four-legged, plant-eating dinosaur with a long neck and tail, such as *Apatosaurus* and *Brachiosaurus*.

Species: A group of living things that are similiar to each other and can interbreed. The basic unit of classification.

Stegosaur ("roofed reptile"): A plant-eating dinosaur with a combination of bony plates and spines along its back and tail.

Theropod ("beast foot"): A two-legged meat-eating dinosaur. Includes tyrannosaurs and birds.

Toxin: A natural poison produced by an organism.

Troodontid ("wounding tooth"): A small theropod dinosaur with large eyes and a relatively big brain.

Tyrannosaur ("tyrant reptile"): A large carnivorous dinosaur from the latter part of the Cretaceous period. Includes *Tyrannosaurus* and its cousins.

INDEX

KINGFISHER
Larousse Kingfisher Chambers Inc.
95 Madison Avenue
New York, New York 10016

First American edition 1994
2 4 6 8 10 9 7 5 3 1

Copyright © Larousse plc 1994

Library of Congress Cataloging-in-Publication Data
Storrs, Glenn William.
Tyrannosaurus/by Glenn Storrs.—1st American ed.
p.   cm.—(Dinoworld)
Includes Index.
1. Tyrannosaurus rex—Juvenile literature.   [1. Tyrannosaurus
rex.   2. Dinosaurs.]   I. Title.   II. Series.
QE862.53576 1994
567.9'7—dc20   93–45531 CIP AC

ISBN 1–85697–993–8

Series Editor: Michèle Byam
Series Designer: Shaun Barlow
Picture Research: Elaine Willis

Dinoventures are written
by Jim Miles

Additional help from Andy Archer, Cathy Tincknell,
Smiljka Surla, Matthew Gore, and Hilary Bird

The publishers would like to thank the following
artists for contributing to the book:
The Apple Illustration Agency, Adrian Chesterman (The Art Collection),
David Cook (Linden Artists), Eugene Fleury, Chris Forsey,
Terry Gabbey (Eva Morris AFA), Bernard Long (Temple Rogers), Luis Rey,
Bernard Robinson, Guy Smith (Mainline Design), Studio Galante

The publishers wish to thank the following
for supplying photographs for the book:
The Natural History Museum, London;
30: American Museum of Natural History, neg. no. 17808;
31: American Museum of Natural History, neg. no. 35923; ZEFA

Printed in Spain